STRUM & SING

Jack Johnson

Cherry Lane Music Company
Director of Publications/Project Editor: Mark Phillips
Publications Coordinator: Gabrielle Fastman

ISBN 1-57560-853-7

Visit our website at www.cherrylane.com

Contents

Banana Pancakes

Words and Music by Jack Johnson

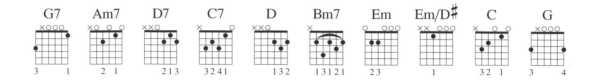

Intro

G7 |Am7 |
Well, can't you see that it's just raining?

Am7 |G7 |
There ain't no need to go out - side.

Verse 1

          D7   ‖G7   D7 |
But baby, you hardly even notice

Am7   C7 |G7
When I try to show you this song,

                D7 |Am7   C7 |
It's meant to keep you from doing what you're s'posed to.

G7   D7 |
Waking up too early,

Am7   C7 |
Maybe we could sleep in.

G7   D7
Make you banana pancakes,

    |Am7   C7 |Am7 |
Pre - tend like it's the weekend now.

Am7 |G7 |
And we could pretend it all the time,   yeah.

G7 |Am7 |
Can't you see that it's just raining?

Am7 |G7 |
There ain't no need to go out - side.

Verse 2

```
G7              D7         ‖G7            D7          |
    But just maybe ha - la ka uku - lele,

Am7           C7
Mama made a baby.

   |G7                      D7
(I) really don't mind the practice,

      |Am7              C7              |
'Cause you're my little lady.

G7           D7
Lady, lady, love me,

      |Am7              C7              |
'Cause I love to lay here, lazy.

G7                       D7
We could close the curtains,

      |Am7              C7       |Am7              |
Pre - tend like there's no world out -    side.

Am7                                |G7          |
    And we could pretend it all the time,  no.

G7                              |Am7            |
    Can't you see that it's just raining?

Am7                                |G7            |
    There ain't no need to go out - side.

G7                          |Am7            |
    Ain't no need, ain't no need.

Am7                         |G7              |
    Mm, mm, mm, mm.

G7                           |Am7            |
    Can't you see, can't you see?

Am7                                |G7          |
    Rain all day and I don't mind.
```

Bridge

‖**Am7** |
But the telephone is singing, ringing;

Am7 |**D** |
It's just too early, don't pick it up.

D
We don't need to;

|**Am7**
We got ev'rything we need right here,

|**Am7** |**D** |
And everything we need is enough.

D |**Bm7** |
(It's) just so easy when the whole world fits in - side of your arms.

|**Em** **Em/D♯** |**C**
Do we really need to pay attention to the alarm?

|**G** |**D7** |**G** |
Wake up slow. Mm, mm. Wake up slow.

Repeat Verse 1

Outro

G7 |**Am7** |
Ain't no need, ain't no need.

Am7 |**G7** |
Rain all day and I real - ly, really, really don't mind.

G7 |**Am7** |
Can't you see, can't you see?

Am7 |**G** ‖
We've got to wake up slow.

Belle

Words and Music by Jack Johnson

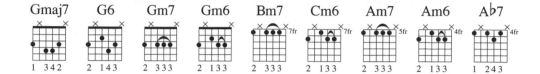

Verse

‖**Gmaj7**   **G6** |
Oi, Li - enda.

|**Gm7**   **Gm6**|
Bella che fa?

|**Gmaj7**   **G6** | |**Bm7**   **Cm6**|
Bo - nita,   bonita, que tal?

|**Am7**   **Am6**|
But belle,

|**Am7**   **A♭7**| |**Gmaj7**   **Cm6**|
Je ne comprends   pas   fran - çais.

|**Am7**   **A♭7**
So you'll have to speak to me,

|**Gmaj7** | ‖
Some other way.

Better Together

Words and Music by Jack Johnson

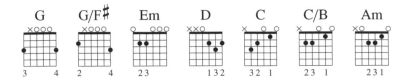

Verse 1

G   G/F♯
There's no combi - nation of words

 |Em   D
I could put on the back of a postcard,

C   C/B
No song that I could sing.

 |Am   D
But I could try for your heart and

G G/F♯ |Em   D
Our dreams, and they are made out of real things,

  |C   C/B
Like a shoebox of photographs

 |Am   D
With sepiatone loving.

G   G/F♯
 Love is the answer,

   |Em   D
At least for most of the questions in my heart,

 |C   C/B |Am
Like, "Why are we here?" and "Where do we go?"

        D
And "How come it's so hard?"

 |G   G/F♯
And it's not always easy,

   |Em   D
And sometimes life can be de - ceiving.

C   C/B
 I'll tell you one thing,

 |Am   D
It's always better when we're to - gether.

Chorus

C |D |

Mm, it's always better when we're together.

C |D |

Yeah, we'll look at the stars when we're together.

C |D |

Well, it's always better when we're together.

C |D   ‖

Yeah, it's always better when we're together.

Interlude

G   G/F♯ |Em   D |C   C/B |Am   D |

G   G/F♯ |Em   D |C   C/B |Am   D

Verse 2

      ‖**G**
And all of these moments

     G/F♯ |**Em**   **D** |
Just might find their way into my dreams tonight,

    |**C**   **C/B**
But I know that they'll be gone

       |**Am**   **D**
When the morning light sings

         |**G**   **G/F♯**
Or brings new things.

      |**Em**   **D**
For to - morrow night you see

    |**C**   **C/B**
That they'll be gone too.

      |**Am**   **D**
Too many things I have to do.

         |**G**   **G/F♯**
But if all of these dreams might find their way

    |**Em**   **D**
Into my day - to - day scene,

    |**C**   **C/B**
I'd be under the impres - sion

    |**Am**   **D** |**G**
I was somewhere in between   with only two,

      G/F♯
Just me and you.

      |**Em**   **D**
Not so many things we got to do

    |**C**   **C/B**
Or places we got to be.

      |**Am**   **D**   ‖
We'll sit be - neath the mango tree now.

Chorus

C |D |
Yeah, it's always better when we're together.

C |D |
Mm, we're somewhere in between together.

C |D |
Well, it's always better when we're together.

C |D ||
Yeah, it's always better when we're together.

Interlude G G/F♯ |Em D |C C/B |Am D |

      G G/F♯ |Em D |C C/B |Am D ||

Bridge

Am |D
 I believe in memo - ries;

     |Am |D
They look so, so pretty when I sleep.

     |Am |D
Hey now, and, and when I wake up,

     |Am
You look so pretty

      |D
Sleeping next to me.

     |C |D
But there is not enough time,

     |C |D
And there is no, no song I could sing.

     |C |D
And there is no combination of words I could say,

     |C |
But I will still tell you one thing:

D ||
 We're better together.

Outro G G/F♯ |Em D |C C/B |Am D |

      G G/F♯ |Em D |C C/B |Am D |G ||

Breakdown

Words and Music by
Jack Johnson, Dan Nakamura and Paul Huston

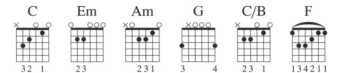

Verse 1

```
C                    |Em              |
      I hope this old train breaks down.

Am                       |G           |
      Then I could take a walk around and

C                    |Em          |
      See what there is to see.

Am                   |G
      Time is just a melody.

                |C
With all the people in the street

      |Em                         |
Walking fast as their feet can take them,

Am                      |G
I   just roll through town.

          |C
And though my window's got a view,

      |Em
Well, the frame I'm looking through

   |Am                        |G          ‖
Seems to have no concern  for me now.   So for now I...
```

Chorus

```
        C     |C/B            |Am              |G            |
        I   need  this here    old train to break down.

        C     |C/B            |Am              |G            ||
        Oh, please just        let me please break down.
```

Interlude

```
        C          |Em      |Am      |G          |
        C          | Em     |Am      |G          ||
```

Verse 2

```
        C                    |Em                |
        Well, this engine screams out loud;

Am                   |G                 |
        Centipede   gonna  crawl westbound.

C                    |Em                  |
        So I don't even  make  a sound, 'cause

Am                           |G
        It's gonna sting me when I leave this town.

           |C                        |Em
And all the people in the street that I'll never get to meet

        |Am                         |
(If) these     tracks don't bend somehow.

G     |C                    |Em
        And I got no time that I    got to get to

        |Am                  |G          ||
Where    I don't need to be.        So I...
```

Repeat Chorus (2x)

Bridge

```
         C   |G       F           |C   |G       F               |
             I wanna break on down.          But I can't stop now.
         C   |G       F           |C        |G       F
             Let me break on down.
```

Verse 3

```
                ||C                      |Em
             But you can't stop nothing if you got no control
                |Am                          |G
             Of the thoughts in your mind that you kept in, you know.
                |C                      |Em
             You don't know nothing, but you don't need to know.
                |Am                      |G
             The wisdom's in the trees, not the glass windows.
                |C                      |Em
             You can't stop wishing if you don't let go,
                |Am                      |G
             The things that you find and you lose and you know.
                |C                      |Em
             You keep on rolling, put the moment on hold.
                |Am                          |G                      ||
             The frame's too bright so put the blinds down low. And...
```

Repeat Chorus (2x)

Outro

```
         C        |Em       |Am       |G


                              |C        |Em       |Am        |G
             I wanna break on down.
                              |C        |Em       |Am       |G       |
             But I can't stop now.
         C        |Em       |Am       |G        |C        ||
```

Cocoon

Words and Music by Jack Johnson

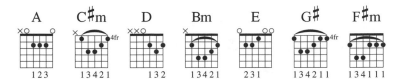

Verse 1

     A |C#m |
Based on your smile,

D   C#m |
I'm betting all of this

Bm |E | |
Might be over soon.

     A |C#m
But you're bound to win,

     |D   C#m |
'Cause if I'm betting against you,

Bm |E | |
I think I'd rather lose.

Bm |E
But this is all that I have.

Chorus

     ‖A   G# |
So please,

D   E |A   G# |
Take what's left of this heart and use,

D   E |A   G# |
Please use only what you really need.

D   E |A   G# |
You know I only have so little, so please,

D   E |A   E |A   E ‖
Mend your broken heart and leave.

Verse 2

```
       A                        |C#m
       I know it's not your style
             |D        C#m              |
And I can  tell by the way that you move
Bm                        |E       |        |
       It's real, real soon.
       A                      |C#m
       But I'm on your side
         |D         C#m               |
And I don't want to be your regret.
Bm                            |E       |       |
       I'd rather be your cocoon.
Bm                               |E
       But this is all that you have.
```

Chorus

```
          ‖A      G#       |
So    please,
D                    E                    |A      G#     |
    Let me take what's left of your heart and I will  use,
D         E           |A    G#    |
    I swear I'll use only what I   need.
D                 E
    I know you only have so little,
     |A       G#      |
So   please,
D                 E                    ‖
    Let me mend my broken heart and….
```

Bridge

A |C#m |
  You said this was all you have   and it's all I need,

F#m |D |
  But blah, blah, blah,   because it fell apart and

A |C#m |
  I guess it's all you knew,   and all I had.

F#m |D
  But now we have   only confused hearts,

   |Bm |E
And   I guess all we have   is really all we need.

Chorus

    ‖A   G# |
So   please,

D   E |A   G# |
Let's take these broken hearts and use,

D   E |A   G# |
Let's use only what we really need.

D   E
You know we only have so little,

  |A   G# |
So, please,

D   E |A   E |A   E |A   ‖
Take these broken hearts and leave.

Bubble Toes

Words and Music by Jack Johnson

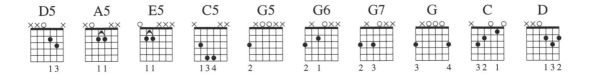

|D5|A5|E5|C5|G5|G6|G7|G|C|D|

Intro

    |D5   A5
It's as simple as something that nobody knows,

        |E5   C5
That her eyes are as big as her bubbly toes,

    |D5   A5
On the feet of a queen of the hearts of the cards,

       |E5   C5 |G5 G6 |G7   G6
And her feet are all covered with tar balls and scars.

    |D5   A5
It's as common as something that nobody knows,

       |E5   C5
That her beauty will follow wher - ever she goes,

    |D5   A5
Up the hill in the back of her house in the…

       |E5
Would she love me forever?

C5 |G5 G6 |G7   G6
I know she could.

    |D5   A5 |
I re - member when you and me,

E5   C5 |D5
  Mm, how we used to be just good friends.

     A5 |
Wouldn't give me none,

E5   C5 |G |C   D |G |C   D ||
But all I wanted was some.

Verse 1

G
She's got a whole lotta reasons,

                 |C   D
She can't think of a single one that can justify leaving.

  |G |C
And he got none, but he thinks he got so many prob - lems,

             |D |G |C   D
Man, he got too much time to waste.

  |G
His dreams are like commercials,

     |C   D
But her dreams are picture per - fect,

     |G
And our dreams are so related,

        |C   D |G |C   D
Though they're often under - estimated.

Chorus

     ‖G
It's as simple as something that nobody knows,

    |C   D
That her eyes are as big as her bub - bly toes,

    |G
On the feet of a queen of the hearts of the cards,

    |C   D |
(And her) feet are infested with tar balls and ...

G |
La, da, da, da, da, da.

C   D |
  La, da, da, da, da, da, da.

G |
La, da, da, da, da, da.

C   D |G |C   D |G |C   D
  La, da, da, da, da, da, da, da.

Verse 2

|G
Well, I was eating lunch at the D.L.G.

    |C   D |
When this little girl came and she sat next to me.

G
Never seen nobody move the way she did.

   |C N.C.
Well, she did and she does and she'll do it again.

     |G
When you move like a jellyfish, rhythm don't mean nothing.

  |C   D |
You go with the flow, you don't stop.

G   N.C.
Move like a jellyfish, rhythm is nothing.

  |C   D |G |C   D
You go with the flow, you don't stop. Mm.

Chorus

    ‖G
It's as common as something that nobody knows,

      |C   D
That her beau - ty will follow wherev - er she goes,

   |G
Up the hill in the back of her house in the wood.

   |C   D |
She'll love me forever, I know   she …

G |
La, da, da, da, da, da.

C   D |
  La, da, da, da, da, da, da.

G |
La, da, da, da, da, da.

C   D |G |
  La, da, da, da, da, da, da, da.

Bridge

‖**G**
If you would only listen,

|**C**   **D**
You might just realize what you're miss - ing,

|**G** |**C**   **D**
You're missing me.

|**G**
If you would only listen,

|**C**   **D**
You might just realize what you're miss - ing,

|**G** |**C**   **D**
You're missing me.

Chorus

‖**G**
It's as simple as something that nobody knows,

|**C**   **D**
That her eyes   are as big as her bub - bly toes,

|**G**
On the feet of a queen of the hearts of the cards,

|**C**   **D** |
(And her) feet are infested with tar   balls and …

G |
La, da, da, da, da, da.

C   **D** |
  La, da, da, da,   da, da, da.

G |
La, da, da, da, da, da.

C   **D** |
  La, da, da, da,   da, da, da.

G |
La, da, da, da, da, da.

C   **D** |
  La, da, da, da,   da, da, da.

G |
La, da, da, da, da, da.

C   **D** |**G** | ‖
  La, da, da, da,   da, da, da, da.

Constellations

Words and Music by Jack Johnson

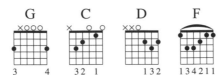

Verse 1

G
   The light was leaving; in the west it was blue.

|C | |
The children's laughter sang,

G
  Skipping just like the stones they threw.

   |C | | | |D | ||
Their voices echoed across the waves.   It's getting late.

Chorus

G |F |
It was   just another night

C |D
    With the sun - set

   |G |F |
And a moonrise not so far behind

C |D
    To give us just enough light

   |G |F |
To lay down underneath the stars,

C |D |
    Listen to Pa - pa's translations

G |F |
Of the stories across the sky.

C |D ||
    We drew our own constellations.

Interlude   G | |C | |G | |C | ||

Verse 2

G |
The west winds often last too long,

   |C | |
And when they calm down, nothing ever feels the same.

G | |
Sheltered under the Ka - mani tree,

C | |
Waiting for the passing rain.

G |
Clouds keep moving to un - cover the sea

   |C | |
Of stars above us, chasing the day away

G | |
To find the stories that we sometimes need.

C | | | |D | ||
Listen close enough,   all else fades,   fades a - way.

Chorus

G |F |
It was   just another night

C |D
With the sun - set

   |G |F |
And a moonrise not so far behind

C |D
To give us just enough light

   |G |F |
To lay down underneath the stars,

C |D |
Listen to all the translations

G |F |
Of the stories across the sky.

C |D |G |F |C |D |G | ||
We drew our own constellations.

Cookie Jar

Words and Music by Jack Johnson

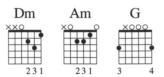

Verse 1

Dm   **Am** |
I would turn on the TV,

G   **Am** |
But it's so embarrassing

Dm   **Am** |
To see all the other people.

G   **Am** ‖
I don't know that they mean.

Verse 2

Dm   **Am** |
And it was magic at first,

G   **Am** |
When   they spoke without sound.

Dm   **Am** |
But now this world is gonna hurt.

G   **Am** |
You better turn that thing down.

Dm **Am** |**G** **Am** ‖
Turn it around.

Verse 3

Dm   Am
"It wasn't me," says   the boy with the gun.

       |G   Am
"Sure, I pulled the trigger but it needed to be done,

        |Dm   Am
Because life's   been killing me ev - er since it begun.

   |G   Am |Dm Am |G   Am
You can't blame me 'cause I'm too young."

Verse 4

   ‖Dm   Am
"You can't blame me. Sure,   the killer was my son,

    |G   Am
But I didn't teach him to pull the trigger of the gun.

    |Dm   Am
It's the   killing on his TV screen.

   |G   Am |Dm Am |G   Am
You can't blame me; it's those images he seen."

Verse 5

   ‖Dm   Am |
"Well, you can't blame me," says   the media man.

G   Am |
"I wasn't the one who came up with the plan.

Dm   Am
I   just point my camera at what the people want to see.

    |G   Am |Dm Am |G   Am
Man, it's a two-way mirror and you can't blame me."

Verse 6

   ‖Dm   Am
"You can't blame me," says   the singer of the song

    |G   Am
Or the maker of the movie which he based his life on.

    |Dm   Am
"It's only entertainment,   as anyone can see.

    |G   Am |Dm Am |G   Am
It's smoke machines and makeup. Man, you can't fool me."

Verse 7

‖Dm   Am
It was you; it was me; it was every man.

  |G   Am
We've all got the blood on our hands.

 |Dm   Am
We only receive what we demand,

  |G   Am |Dm Am |G Am ‖
And if we want hell, then hell's what we'll have.

Verse 8

Dm Am |
 I would turn on the TV,

G Am |
 But it's so embarrassing

Dm Am |
 To see all the other people

G Am   ‖
 Don't even know what they mean.

Verse 9

Dm Am |
 And it was magic at first,

G Am |
 But let everyone down.

Dm Am |
 And now this world is gonna hurt.

G Am |
 You better turn it around.

Dm Am |G Am |Dm   ‖
     Turn it around.

Cupid

Words and Music by Jack Johnson

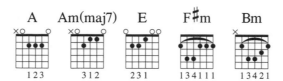

Verse

|A   Am(maj7) |E   F♯m
Well, how man - y times must we go   through this?

|A   Am(maj7) |E   F♯m |
You always been mine, woman; I thought you   knew this.

A   Am(maj7) |E   F♯m
 How man - y times must we go   through this?

|A   Am(maj7) |E   F♯m |Bm |E
You always be mine; Cupid on - ly   misses some - times.

|A   Am(maj7) |E   F♯m |
Mm,   hmm.

|A   Am(maj7) |E   F♯m
Mm,   hmm.

Chorus

‖Bm |E
But we could end up brokenhearted

|A   Am(maj7) |F♯m
If   we don't remember   why   all this all started.

|Bm |E
And if   they try to tell you love fades with time,

|A   Am(maj7) |F♯m
Tell them   there's no such thing as time.

|Bm   E |A   Am(maj7) |
It's our   time.   It's our   time.

E   F♯m |A   Am(maj7) |E   F♯m |A   ‖
   It's our   time.   It's our   time.

Crying Shame

Lyrics by Jack Johnson
Music by Jack Johnson and Adam Topol

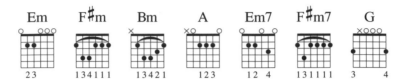

Intro

       Em   **|F♯m**   **|Em**
                          It's such a tired game.

        |F♯m
Will it ever stop?

               |Em
How will this all play out of sight,

        |F♯m   **‖**
Out of mind, now?

Verse 1

F♯m |
By now we should know how to com - municate

                                         |Bm
Instead of coming to blows. We're on a roll,

   A |Bm
And there ain't no stopping us now.

    A |Bm
We're   burning under con - trol.

A |Bm   A |F♯m
  Isn't it strange how we're all burning under the same sun?

                     |
Buy now and save; it's a war for peace.

F♯m
   It's the same old game,

                  |Bm
But do we really want to play?

   A |Bm
We could close our eyes; it's still there.

   A |Bm
We could say it's us against them.

   A |
We could try but nobody wins.

Bm   A   ‖Em7
  Grav - ity has got a hold on us all.

Pre-Chorus

|F♯m7 |Em7

Could try to put it out,   but it's a growing flame.

|F♯m7 |Em7

Using fear as fuel,   burning down our name.

|F♯m7 |Em7

And it won't take too long, 'cause words all burn the same.

|F♯m7

And who we gonna blame   now? And oh,

Chorus

‖Bm   A |G   F♯m

It's such a cry - ing, cry - ing, cry - ing   shame.

|Bm   A |G   F♯m

It's such a cry - ing, cry - ing, cry - ing   shame.

|Bm   A |G   F♯m |Em | ‖

It's such a cry - ing, cry - ing, cry - ing   shame,   shame,   shame.

Interlude   Bm   A |Bm   A |Bm   A |Bm   A   ‖

Verse 2

F♯m
By now it's beginning to show;

|**F♯m** |**Bm**
A number of people are numbers that ain't coming home.

    A |**Bm**
I could close my eyes, it's still there;

A |
Close my mind, be alone.

Bm **A** |**Bm**
I could close my heart and not care,

       A |**F♯m**
But grav - ity has got a hold on us all.

                    |
It's a terrific price to pay.

F♯m |
  But in the true sense of the word,

Bm   **A** |
Are we using what we've learned?

Bm   **A** |
In the true sense of the word,

Bm   **A** |
Are we losing what we were?

Bm   **A**   ‖**Em7**
It's such a tired game.

Pre-Chorus

    |**F♯m7** |**Em7**
Will it ever stop? It's not for me to say.

      |**F♯m7** |**Em7**
And is it in our blood, or is it just our fate?

       |**F♯m7** |**Em7**
And how will this all play out of sight, out mind, now?

      |**F♯m7**
Who we gonna blame, all in all?

Repeat Chorus

Do You Remember

Words and Music by Jack Johnson

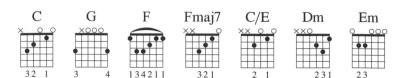

Verse 1

     ‖**C** | |
Do you re - member   when   we first met?

G | |**F** | |**C** |
I sure do.   It was some - time in   early Sep - tember.

G |**C** | |**G** |
  Well, you were lazy about   it; you made me wait around.

    |**F** | |**C** |
I was so crazy about   you, I didn't mind.

G |**C** | |**G** |
  So I was late for   class;   I locked my bike to yours.

    |**F** | |**C** |**G**
It wasn't hard to find;   you painted flowers on it.

    |**C** | |**G** |
Guess that I was afraid   that if you rolled away

    |**F** | |**C**   **G**
You might not roll back my direc - tion real soon.

Chorus

    ‖**G** |
Well, I was crazy 'bout   you then

    |**G** |
And now, but the cra - ziest thing of all,

|**Fmaj7** |**C/E** |**Dm** |
Over ten   years have gone   by

Dm | | | |
  And you're still mine.   We're locked in time.

Dm |**G** |**F** |**Em** |
  Let's re - wind.

Verse 2

```
Dm                    ‖C                    |                    |G              |
      Do you re - member when    we first moved in togeth - er?
                      |F            |          |C              |
The pi - ano took up the living room.
G              |C            |          |G                  |
   You'd play me boogie - woog - ie; I'd play you love   songs.
                      |F              |          |C              |
You'd say we're playing   house;      now you still say we are.
G              |C            |          |G              |
   We built our getaway    up in a tree we found.
               |F          |          |C              |
We felt so far away,       but we were still in town.
G              |C            |          |G              |
   Now, I re - member   watch - ing   that old tree burn down.
               |F          |          |C        |G
I took a picture that    I don't like to look at.
```

Chorus

```
         ‖G                  |
Well, all these times, they come and go,

         |G                  |
And alone   don't seem so long.

         |Fmaj7      |C/E         |Dm          |
Over ten   years   have gone by.
Dm              |          |          |          |
   We can't re - wind.      We're locked in time.
Dm              |G          |F        |Em          |
   But you're still  mine.
Dm              |C          ‖
   Do you re - member?
```

Dreams Be Dreams

Words and Music by Jack Johnson

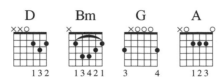

Verse 1

D   Bm |G   A |
She's just waiting for the sum - mertime, when the weath - er's fine.

D   Bm |G   A
She could hitch a ride   out of town and so far away

             |D   Bm |G   A
From that low - down,   good for noth - ing,

      |D   Bm |G
Mis - take - making fool with ex - cuses like,

Chorus

A   ‖D |Bm
"Baby, that was a long   time ago."

   |G |
But that's just a euphemism.

A
If you want the truth,

      |D |Bm
He was out   of control.

   |G |
But a short time's a long time

A   ‖
When your mind just won't let it go.

Verse 2

D   Bm |G   A
   Well, summer came a - long and then it was gone and so was she;

|D   Bm |G   A
But not from him, 'cause he followed her just to let her know

|D   Bm |
Her dreams are dreams

G   A |D   Bm |
  And all this living's so much harder than it seems.

G   A |D   Bm |
  But, girl, don't let your dreams be dreams.

G   A |D   Bm |
  You know this living's not so hard as it seems.

G   A |D Bm |G   A |D Bm |G   A
Don't let your dreams   be dreams,

|D Bm |G A |D Bm |G A |D ||
Your dreams   be dreams,   be dreams.

Drink the Water

Words and Music by Jack Johnson

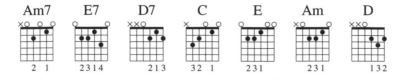

Verse 1

Am7 |
Drink the water, drink it down.

Am7
    This time I know I'm bound

|**E7** |
To spit it back up.

D7 |**Am7** |
  I didn't want this salty substitute;

Am7
    Just not goin' to do.

 |**E7** |
I need some air

D7 |**Am7** |
  If I'm going to live through this experience.

Am7 |**E7** |
    Reminds me of a clock that just won't tick.

D7 |
I want to wake up

Am7 |
From this concussion,

Am7
    But my dream is just not done.

 |**E7** |
I'm late again.

D7 |**Am7**
  It's just one of those bad days.

     |**Am7**
Look outside and   be careful what you ride.

 |**E7** |**D7**   ‖
You just might find   that you're out of...

Chorus

```
C              |E        |Am           |
Time  to  swim       ashore.

Am        |C                  |
    If  I  drift      long  enough,

E                       |Am       |        ‖
      I'll  be  home.
```

Verse 2

```
Am7                         |
    He's  got  delusions  between   his  ears,

              |E7                |D7       |
Man,  it  takes    up  too  much  space.

Am7                      |
    And  all  that  tension  between   his  gears,

             |E7               |D7
Man,  he'll  nev - er  ever  leave  this  place.

        |Am7
He's  got  stones  instead  of  bones,

     |Am7               |
And  everybody  knows,

E7                         |D7
   Ah,  man,  that  can  make  you  real,  real  slow.

       |Am7
And  if  heaven  was  below,

            |Am7              |
IIe'd  know  just  where  to  go.

E7
   Dive  in  the  ocean,

           |D7                         ‖
And  he'd  sink  like  a  stone,  and  he'd  say,
```

Chorus

```
        C               |E        |Am        |
        "It's time to swim   ashore.

        Am          |C                    |
           If I drift       long enough,

        E          |Am        |           ||
         I'll  be  home."
```

Bridge

```
        Am
        Hold  on  if  you  can;

                    |Am
        You're gonna sink faster

                        |E            |D
        Than  you  can  imag - ine, so hold.

                |Am
        Ah,  just  hold  on  if  you  can;

                    |Am
        You're gonna sink faster

                        |E            |D
        Than  you  can  imag - ine, so hold.
```

Chorus

```
                    ||C       |E       |Am        |
        It's just time     to swim      ashore.

        Am          |C              |
           If I drift       long enough,

        E          |Am        ||
          I'll  be  home.
```

Flake

Words and Music by Jack Johnson

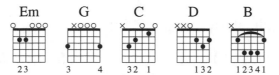

Verse 1

Em | G |
I know she said it's al - right,

C | G |
But you can make it up next time.

Em | G |
I know she knows it's not right;

C | G |
There ain't no use in ly - ing.

Em | G
Maybe she thinks I know something,

| C | G |
Maybe, may - be she thinks it's fine.

Em | G
Maybe she knows something I don't.

| C | D ‖
I'm so, I'm so tired, I'm so tired of trying.

Chorus

```
     G                          |D           |
    It seems to me that "may - be,"
     Em                             |B            |
      It pretty much always means   "no."
          |C          |D                  |G      |D        |
    So don't  tell me you might; just let it go.
     G                        |D          |
     And oftentimes we're la - zy;
     Em                          |B
      It seems to stand in my   way.
         |C                    |D
    'Cause no one, no, not no   one
                          |G        |D        ‖
    Likes to be let down.
```

Verse 2

```
     Em                       |G           |
    I know she loves the sun - rise,
     C                      |G                  |
      No longer sees it with her sleeping eyes and...
     Em                             |G
      I know that when she said she's gonna try,
             |C                  |G              |
    Well, it might   not work because of other ties and....
     Em                            |G         |
      I know she usually has some other ties, and
     C                           |G                                 |
      I wouldn't want to break 'em, nah,  I wouldn't want to break 'em.
     Em                       |G
      Maybe she'll help me to untie this,
         |C              |D                          ‖
    But  until then, well,    I'm gonna have to lie, too.
```

Repeat Chorus

```
G                                    |D          |
...It seems to me that "may - be,"

Em                               |B
    It pretty much always means "no."

        |C            |D              |G        |D
So don't  tell me you might; just let it go.
```

```
               ‖G                                      |C
Outro          (The) harder that you try, baby, the further you'll fall,

                    |G                |D              |
Even with all  the money in the whole  wide world.

G                               |
Please, please, please don't pass me...

C                               |
Please, please, please don't pass me...

D          C              |G
Please, please, please don't pass me by.

        |G                                              |C
Everything you know about me now, baby, you gonna have to change,

                |G                      |D              |
You gonna have to call  it by a brand-new name,  oo, oo, oo.

G                               |
Please, please, please don't drag me...

C                               |
Please, please, please don't drag me...

D          C              |G
Please, please, please don't drag me down.

        |G                                              |C
Just like a tree  down by the water, baby, I shall not move,

        |G                |D              |
Even after all the silly things you do, oo, oo, oo,

G                               |
Please, please, please don't drag me...

C                               |
Please, please, please don't drag me...

D          C              |G        |        ‖
Please, please, please don't drag me down.
```

Fall Line

Words and Music by Jack Johnson

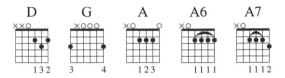

Verse 1

D
   And by the way, you know that hope will make you strange,

  |D
Make you blink, make you blank, make you sink.

     |G
It will make you a - fraid of change

   |G
And of - ten blame the box with the view of the world

G   **|D**
   And the ones that fill the frame. I turn it up,

  |D
But then I turn it off, because I   can't stand

D   **|G**
When they start to talk about the hurting and killing.

   |G
Whose shoes are we filling? The damage and ruin, man,

  |G
The things that we're doing, God.

D
  We gotta stop, we gotta turn it all off;

   |D
We gotta rewind, (and) start it up again,

Chorus

          ║**A** |**A6** |
Because we fell across the fall   line.

A7 |**A6** |**G** | |
    Ain't there nothing sa - cred anymore?

          |**G** |**D** |**G** |**D** |**G**
Na, na, na, na, na, na, na, na.

Verse 2

          ║**D** |
Some - body saw him jump, yeah, but nobody saw him slip.

          |**D** |
I guess he lost a lot of hope, and then he lost his grip.

          |**G** | |
And now he's lying in the freeway in the middle of this mess.

G | |
Guess we lost another one, just like the other one.

D |
Optimistic hypocrite that didn't have the nerve to quit

          |**D** |
The things that kept him wanting more un - til he fin'lly reached the core.

Chorus

          ║**A** |**A6** |
He fell across the fall   line.

A7 |**A6** |**G** | |
    Ain't there nothing sa - cred anymore?

          |**G** |**D**   ║
Na, na, na, na, na, na, na, na.

Fortunate Fool

Words and Music by Jack Johnson

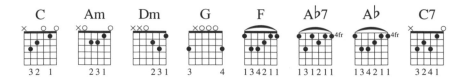

Verse 1

C   Am |C   Am |
She's got it all   figured out;

C   Am |C   Am |
She knows what ev - 'rything's about.

C   Am |Dm
And when   anybody doubts   her

       |G |Dm   G
Or sings songs without   her,

      |C   Am |C   Am ||
She's just so… Mm.

Verse 2

C   Am |C   Am |
She knows the world   is just her stage,

C   Am |C   Am |
And so she'll nev - er misbehave.

C   Am |Dm
She gives thanks   for what they gave   her.

    G |Dm   G
Man, they practic'lly made   her

   |C   Am |C   Am
Into a… Mm.

  |F
But she's the one that stumbles when she talks about

  |G
The seven foreign films that she's checked out.

Chorus

```
        ‖C                Am        |G        F
Such a      fortunate fool.

              |C            Am        |G            F
She's just too   good to be true.

            |C          Am        |G        F
She's such a    fortunate fool.

            |C        Am      |A♭7        F      ‖
She's just so… Mm.
```

Interlude

```
C    Am    |C    Am    |C    Am    |C    Am    ‖
```

Verse 3

```
C                Am            |C    Am      |
   She's got it all     figured out;

C                    Am              |C    Am      |
   She knows what ev - 'rything's about.

C          Am            |Dm
   And when     anybody doubts     her

     |G            |Dm        G
Or sings songs about     her,

            |C      Am    |C      Am      |
She's just so… Mm.

     |F
But she's the one that stumbles when she talks about…

     |G        N.C.
So maybe we shouldn't talk about…
```

Outro

```
        ‖C          Am        |G        F
Such a      fortunate fool.

              |C            Am        |G        F
She's just too   good to be true.

            |C          Am        |G        F
She's such a    fortunate fool.

            |C        Am      |A♭        |      F    |C7          ‖
She's just so… Mm.
```

F-Stop Blues

Words and Music by Jack Johnson

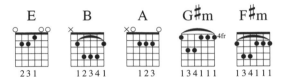

Verse 1

    E   B
  Hermit crabs and cow - ry shells

            |A
Crush be - neath his feet as he comes towards you.

    |E   B |A
He's   wav - ing at you.

     |E   B |
Lift him up to see what you can see.

  A
  He begins his focusing.

    |E   B |
He's   aim - ing at you.

  A |E   B
    And now he has cutaways from mem - ories

   |A |
And   close-ups of anything that

E   B |
  He has seen or e - ven dreamed.

A
  And now he's finished focusing.

    |E   B |
He's imagining lightning

A |
  Striking sea sickness

E   B |A ||
Away from here.

Chorus

```
          E                           G♯m
          Look who's laughing now,

                        |A        B         |
          That you've    wast - ed,

          E                 G♯m         |A                B            |
          How many years?        And you've barely even tast - ed

          E                    G♯m              |
          Anything remote -    ly close to

          A                       B              |
          Everything you've boast - ed about.

          E                        G♯m        |A      B      ‖
          Look who's crying now.
```

Verse 2

```
          E                     B                  |
           Driftwood floats after years of erosion.

          A                                         |
          Incoming tide touches roots to expose them.

          E                 B              |
           Quicksand steals my   shoes.

          A                           |
           Clouds bring the f-stop blues.

          F♯m              |A               ‖
```

Repeat Chorus

Gone

Words and Music by Jack Johnson

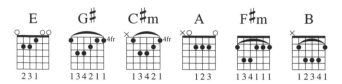

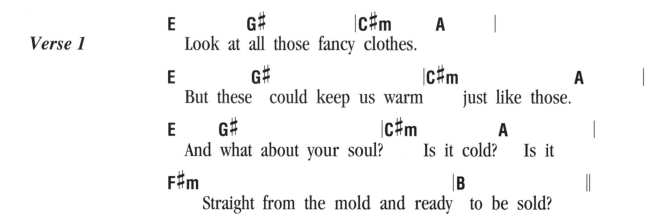

Verse 1

E   G♯ |C♯m   A |
Look at all those fancy clothes.

E   G♯ |C♯m   just like those.   A |
But these could keep us warm

E   G♯ |C♯m   A |
And what about your soul?   Is it cold?   Is it

F♯m |B   ‖
Straight from the mold and ready to be sold?

Verse 2

E   G♯ |C♯m A |
And cars and phones and diamond rings;   bling, bling.

E   G♯ |C♯m   A |
Those are only remov - able things.

E   G♯ |C♯m   A |
And what about your mind?   Does it shine   or

F♯m |B   ‖
Are there things that concern you more than your time?

Chorus

```
     E        B        |C#m           A
       Gone, going, gone,      everything gone.

        |E          B                  |C#m                A
     Give a damn. Gone be the birds when  they don't want to sing.

        |E     B  |C#m                      A     |E   C#m  |E   C#m  ||
     Gone people,   all awkward with their things.   gone.
```

Verse 3

```
     E         G#              |C#m      A        |
       Look at you, out to make a deal.

     E         G#                  |C#m            A             |
       You try to be appealing, but you lose your appeal.

     E     G#                |C#m            A
     And what about those shoes     you're in today?

                       |F#m                    |B                    ||
     They'll do no good      on the bridges you burnt along the way, oh.
```

Chorus

```
     E        B        |C#m        A                     |
       You're willing to sell     anything.  Gone with your herd.

     E          B                 |C#m                        A
       Leave your footprints (and) we'll shame them with our words.

        |E       B    |C#m            A              ||
     Gone people,    all careless and con - sumed.  Gone.
```

Chorus

```
     E        B        |C#m      A
       Gone,  going, gone,     everything gone.

        |E          B            |C#m                   A
     Give a damn. Gone be the birds if they don't wanna sing.

        |E     B  |C#m              A        |E            ||
     Gone people,    all awkward with their things.  Gone.
```

Good People

Words and Music by Jack Johnson

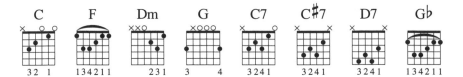

Verse 1

C   F |Dm
Well, you win; it's your show   now.

G
So what's it gonna be?

C   F |
'Cause people   will tune in.

Dm   G |
How many train wrecks do we need to see

C   F |
Before   we lose touch?

Dm   G |
Oh, and we thought this was low.

C   F |Dm
Well, it's bad, gettin' worse,   oh.

Chorus

```
G                        ‖C      F      |
```
Where'd all the good people go?

```
Dm              G
```
I've been changing channels;

```
        |C                  F            |
```
I don't   see them on the T - V shows.

```
Dm    G                        |C    F      |
```
Where'd all the good people go?

```
Dm        G                    |C      F      |Dm    G
```
We got heaps and heaps of what   we sow.

Verse 2

```
        ‖C                  F
```
They got this and that with a rattle a tat.

```
        |Dm              G
```
Testing,   one, two. Man, what - cha gonna do?

```
    |C                F              |
```
Bad news, misused, got too much to lose.

```
Dm                        G
```
Gimme some truth. Now who's   side are we on?

```
        |C            F
```
What - ever you say.

```
        |Dm            |G
```
Turn on the boob tube; I'm in the mood to obey.

```
    |C            F
```
So lead me astray.

```
            |Dm
```
And by the way   now...

Repeat Chorus

Bridge

F |C7   C#7 |
 Sitting 'round, feeling far away. Yeah.

D7 |G
 So far away, but I can feel the de - bris.

     Gb |
Can you feel it?

F |C7   C#7 |
 You interrupt me from a friendly conversation

D7 |G Gb |
 To tell me how great it's all gonna be.

F |C7   C#7
 You might no - tice some hesitation,

    |D7
'Cause it's important to you;

       |G
It's not important to me.

       Gb |
Mm, mm, mm, mm.

F |C7   C#7 |
 Way down by the edge of your reason,

D7
 Well, it's beginning to show,

 |F
And all I really wanna know is…

Repeat Chorus

Verse 3

   ‖**C**   **F**
They got this and that with a rattle a tat.

        |**Dm**   **G**
Testing,   one, two. Man, what - cha gonna do?

   |**C**   **F**
Bad news, misused, give me some truth.

      |**Dm**
You got too much to lose.

     G |**C**
Who's side are we on today, anyway?

         F |
Okay, what - ever you say,

Dm   **G** |
Wrong or resolute but in the mood to obey.

C   **F** |**Dm**   **G** |
Station to sta - tion, desensi - tizing the na - tion.

C   ‖
Going, going, gone.

Holes to Heaven

Words and Music by Jack Johnson

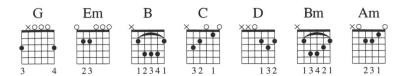

Verse 1

|G
The air was more than human

|G
And the heat   was more than hungry,

|G |Em |
And the cars   were square and spitting diesel fumes.

|G
The bulls were running wild

|G
Because they're big and mean and sacred,

|G |Em |
And the chil - dren were playing cricket with no shoes.

Pre-Chorus

‖B | |
The next morning we woke up, man, with a seven-hour drive.

C
There we were stuck in Port Blaire,

|C   ‖
Where boats break and children stare.

Chorus

```
          G                    D
There were so many   fewer questions

       |Em            Bm                       |C        Bm              |Am
When      stars were still    just the holes to heav - en.        Mm, hmm.

       |G              D
And   there were so many  fewer questions

       |Em            Bm                       |C        Bm
When      stars were still    just the holes to heav - en.

       |Am                         |G      |        |        |        ‖
Mm.                     Mm, mm.
```

Verse 2

```
          G
Disembarking from the port,

          |G                                  |
With no    mistakes of any sort.

          G                                           |Em           |
Moving south, the engine running smooth.

          |G
Of - ficials were quite friendly

                      |G
Once we drowned    them with our sweet talk

              |G                                          |Em          |
And we bribed    them with our cigarettes and booze.
```

Pre-Chorus

```
          ‖B                                    |                        |
The next morning we woke up, man, with the sunrise to the right,

          C
Moving back north to Port Blaire,

          |C                            ‖
Where boats break and children stare.
```

Repeat Chorus

The Horizon Has Been Defeated

Words and Music by Jack Johnson

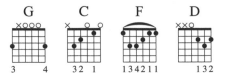

Verse 1

        |G   C
(The) ho - rizon has been defeat - ed

     |F   G |
By the pirates of the new age.

G   C
Alien casi - nos,

   |F   G
Well, maybe it's just time to say

   |G   C
That things can go bad

   |F   G
And make you want to run away.

   |G |C
But as we grow old - er,

 |F |D | ‖
The trouble just seems to   stay.

Verse 2

    G   C
Future complica - tions

      |F   G
In the strings between the cans.

    |G   C
But no prints can come from fin - gers

     |F   G
If ma - chines become our hands.

      |G   C
And then our feet become the wheels,

      |F   G
And then the wheels become the cars.

      |G   C
And then the rigs begin to drill

      |F |D | ||
Until the drilling goes too   far.

Chorus

    G   C
Things can go bad

    |F   G
And make you want to run away.

   |G   C
But as we grow old - er,

     |F |D   C |G |D   C |G ||
(The) ho - rizon begins to   fade, fade, fade,   fade away.

Verse 3

G   C |
Thingamajigsaw puz - zled;

F   G |
Anger, don't you step too close.

    |G
'Cause people are lonely

    C |F   G |
And on - ly ani - mals with fancy shoes.

G   C |
Hallelujah zig zag noth - ing;

F   G
Misery, it's on the loose.

    |G
'Cause people are lonely

    C |F |
And on - ly ani - mals with too many tools

D |
  That can build all the junk that we sell.

D ||
Oh, sometime, man, make you want to yell, and....

Chorus

G   C
Things can go bad

 |F   G
And make you want to run away.

 |G   C
But as we grow old - er,

    |F |D C |G |D C |G |
(The) ho - rizon begins to fade away,   fade away.

D C |G |
 Fade, fade, fade.

D C |G ||
 Fade, fade, fade.

Inaudible Melodies

Words and Music by Jack Johnson

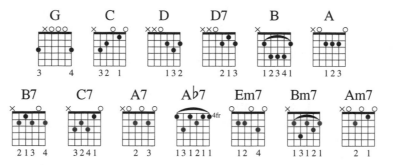

Verse 1

|G
Brushfire fairytales,

|C
Itsy bitsy diamond whales.

|G
Big fat hurricanes,

|C
Yellow-bellied given names.

|D
Well, shortcuts can slow you down.

|C
And in the end   we're bound

|G |D
To rebound off of we.

Verse 2

        ‖**G**
Well, dust off your thinking caps,

      |**C**
Solar powered plastic plants.

     |**G**
Pretty pictures of things we ate,

      |**C**
We are only what   we hate.

      |**D**
But in the long run we have found

      |**C**
Silent films are full of sound,

   |**G** |**D7**   ‖
Inaudibly free.

Chorus

G
Slow down, everyone,

  |**B** |
You're moving too fast.

C
Frames can't catch you when

  |**A**   ‖
You're moving like that.

Bridge 1

G
Inaudible melodies

  |**B** |
Serve narrational strategies.

C
Unobtrusive tones

   |**A**
Help to notice nothing but the zone

  |**G** |
Of visual relevancy.

B |
Frame-lines tell me what to see,

C
Chopping like an axe,

   |**A** ||
Or maybe Eisenstein should just relax.

Repeat Chorus

Bridge 2

  ||**G**
Well, Plato's cave is full of freaks

  |**B7**
De - manding refunds for the things they've seen.

 |**C7**
I wish they could believe

   |**A7**   **A♭7** ||
In all the things   that never made the screen. And just

Repeat Chorus

Outro   **G**   **D7** |**Em7**   **Bm7** |**C**   **Bm7** |**Am7** |**G** ||

If I Could

Words and Music by Jack Johnson

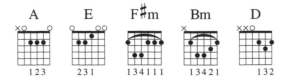

Verse 1

```
         A              E          |F♯m
         A  brand-new  baby  was  born  yesterday

Bm             |A    E    |F♯m  Bm    |
   Just  in  time.

         A              E              |
         Papa  cried,    baby  cried,

F♯m                    Bm         |A    E    |F♯m    Bm    |
        Said, "Your  tears    are  like  mine."

         A              E          |F♯m
         I  heard  some  words  from  a  friend  on  the  phone;

Bm           |A    E    |F♯m  Bm    |
Didn't  sound  so  good.

         A          E          |F♯m
         The  doctor  gave  him  two  weeks  to  live;

Bm                     |E                  ||
   I'd  give  him  more      if  I  could.
```

Chorus

   A D |Bm E |A D |
       You know that I would now,

Bm E |A D |
   If only I could.

Bm   E |A D |
   You know that I would now,

Bm   E   ‖
   If only I could.

Interlude   A E |F♯m Bm |A E |F♯m Bm ‖

Verse 2

   A   E |F♯m
   Down the mid - dle drops one more

Bm |A E |F♯m Bm
   Grain of sand.

     |A   E |F♯m Bm |A E |F♯m Bm|
They say that new life makes losing life eas - ier to under - stand.

A   E |F♯m
   Words are kind; they help ease the mind.

   Bm |A E |F♯m Bm
I'll miss my old friend.

      |A   E
And though you've gotta go,

     |F♯m   Bm
We'll keep a piece of your soul.

     |E   ‖
One goes out,   one comes in.

Repeat Chorus

It's All Understood

Words and Music by Jack Johnson

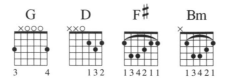

Intro

```
G                D            |
Da, na, na, na, na.

F#               Bm           |
Da, na, na, na, na,      na.

G                D            |
Da, na, na, na, na.

F#               Bm           ‖
Da, na, na, na, na,      na.
```

Verse 1

```
 G                          D
Everyone laughed at her joke,

      |F#                        Bm
As if they'd never even heard it before.

   |G                        D
And maybe they were truly amused,

    |F#                          Bm
But every word that she spoke was a bore.

   |G                        D
And maybe it's because they had seen

    |F#                       Bm
The previews on the TV screen.

    |G                           D
Well, this part is good and that's well   understood,

        |F#                         Bm
So you should laugh, if you know what I mean.
```

Chorus

```
              ‖G           D           |
But it's all relative,

F♯                              Bm
Even if you don't understand.

                   |G           D
Well, it's all understood,

     |F♯                              Bm
Es - pecially when you don't understand.

                    |G           D           |
Then it's all just because,

F♯                              Bm
Even if we don't understand,

                    |G     D    |F♯   Bm  |G     D    |F♯   Bm  ‖
Then let's all just believe.
```

Verse 2

```
G                              D
Everyone knows what went down,

        |F♯                              Bm
Because the news was spread all over town.

   |G                         D
And fact is only what you believe,

   |F♯                              Bm
And fact and fiction work as a team.

        |G                              D
It's almost always fiction in the end, that content begins to bend

        |F♯                              Bm
When context is never the same.
```

Repeat Chorus

Verse 3

```
          G                        D
      I was reading a book,

      |F#                          Bm
   Or maybe it was a magazine.

          |G                       D
   Sug - gestions on where to place faith.

          |F#                      Bm
   Sug - gestions on what to believe.

          |G                              D
   But I read somewhere that you've got  to beware.

          |F#                     Bm
   You can't believe anything you read.

           |G                            D
   But the Good Book is good, and that's well  understood,

              |F#
   So don't even question,

                             Bm
   If you know what I mean.
```

Repeat Chorus

Outro

```
          ‖G         D
      But there you go once again.

          |F#
   You missed the point,

       Bm                |G        D          |
   And then you point your fingers at me

   F#   Bm                         |G     D     |F#
      And say that I said not to believe.

   Bm          |G
      Ah, but there you go once again.
```

D
You missed the point,

                |F#
And then you point your fingers at me,

      Bm   **|G**
And you say that I said not to believe.

D   **|F#**
  But I be - lieve.

Bm   **|G**
   Ah, but there you go once again.

      D
You missed the point,

                |F#
And then you point your fingers at me,

      Bm   **|G**
And you say that I said not to believe.

D   **|F#**   **Bm**   **|G**
  But I be - lieve.

D   **|**
  I guess,

F#   **Bm**   **|**
  I guess it's all   relative.

G   **D**   **|**
Da, na, na, na, na.

F#   **Bm**   **|**
Da, na, na, na, na,   na.

G   **D**   **|**
Da, na, na, na, na.

F#   **Bm**   **|**
Da, na, na, na, na,   na.

G   **D**   **|**
Da, na, na, na, na.

F#   **Bm**   **|G**   **‖**
Da, na, na, na, na,   na. Da.

Losing Hope

Words and Music by Jack Johnson

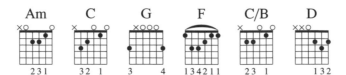

Verse 1

       |**Am**   **C**   **G**
I got a faulty parachute. I got a stranger's friend,

       |**Am**   **C**   **G**
An ex - citing change in my butcher's blend,

      |**Am**   **C**   **G**
A symbol on the ceiling with the flick of a switch,

       |**Am**   **C**   **G** |**F** |
Yeah, my new-found hero in the enemy's ditch,   yeah.

Verse 2

       ‖**Am**   **C**   **G**
Well, somebody's something was left in the room,

      |**Am**   **C**   **G**
And now that it's gone, well, of course we assume

      |**Am**   **C**   **G**
That somebody else needed some - thing so bad,

      |**Am**   **C**   **G** |**F** | ‖
They took ev'rything that somebody had.

Chorus

```
      C            C/B      |Am                |
      Losing hope   is eas - y

      D                     G
      When your only friend    is gone,

         |D                 G              |
      And  every time you look    around,

      D              G                      |C       C/B       |
       Well, it all, it all   just seems to change.

      |Am      C  G  |Am      C  G  |Am      C  G  |Am      C  G
```

Verse 3

```
         ‖Am                      C              G
      The mark was left; man, it's nev - er the same.

            |Am                   C              G           |
      Next time    that you shoot, make sure that you aim.

      Am                    C       G
      Open windows with pass - ing cars,

      |Am                   C    G  |F         |          ‖
      A brand-new night with the same old stars.
```

Repeat Chorus

Verse 4

```
        G        ‖Am   C   G       |Am
Feed the fool         a piece of the pie.

C       G        |Am      C       G          |Am
  Make a fool of his sys - tem.      Make a fool of his mind.

C       G          |Am   C    G        |Am
  Give him bottles of lies,      and maybe he'll    find

C       G        |Am      C         G        |Am   C  G  |F   |      ‖
  His place in heav - en,      because he might just die.
```

Repeat Chorus

```
         |C        C/B    |Am           |
... But hanging on    is eas - y,

D                        G
When you've got a friend  to call.

    |D            G              |
When nothing's making sense at all,

D                    G              |C      C/B    |
  You're not the only one  who's afraid of change.

Am   C  G  |Am   C  G  |Am   C  G  |Am   C  G  |Am        ‖
```

Middle Man

Words and Music by Jack Johnson

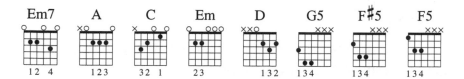

Verse 1

|Em7
Well, he's not necessarily trying to say that he minds it,

|A
But someone plays evil tricks on that kid.

|Em7
Yeah, he's not necessarily trying to say God can't be trusted,

|A
Yeah, but someone plays evil tricks on that kid.

|Em7
And certain situations scream for deviations,

|A
But somehow he always gets stuck in the middle

|Em7
Of this and that and, man, he should try less

|A
Every time he's rejected, man, he loses affection.

|C
But don't wc all, don't we just got to give a little time? |

A   D
Maybe give a friend a call instead of making him

Chorus

    ‖**Em**   **D** |
Con - fused.

A   **D** |**Em**   **D** |
What a terrible thing for you to do.

A   **D** |**Em**   **D** |
What an awful thing for you to say.

A   **D** |**A** |**G5** **F♯5** **F5** |
What a terrible thing for you to re - lay.

Em |**A** |**Em** |**A**

Verse 2

    ‖**Em7**
Well, I know some peoples, they got a little less than nothing,

   |**A** |
Yeah, but still find some to spare

Em7 |
And other people got more than they could use,

A |
But they don't share.

Em7
And some people got problems, man,

   |**A** |
They got awful complications.

Em7 |**A**
Other people got perfect situa - tions

With no provocation.

  |**C** |
But don't we all, don't we just got to give a little time?

A   **D**
Maybe give a friend a call instead of making him

Chorus

```
      ‖Em              D              |
Con - fused.

  A                D                |Em    D       |
  What a terrible thing for you to do.

  A                D                |Em    D       |
  What an awful thing for you to say.

  A                D
  What a terrible thing for you.

              |Em    D       |
Confused.

  A                D                |Em    D       |
  What a terrible thing for you to do.

  A                D                |Em    D       |
  What an awful thing for you to say.

  A                D                |A          |G5    F#5    F5    |
  What a terrible thing for you to re - lay.

  Em         |A         |Em         |A
```

Outro

```
      ‖Em              |
Con - fused.

  A                              |Em        |A
  What an awful thing for you to do.

      |Em              |
Con - fused.

  A                              |Em    |A       |Em          ‖
  What an awful thing for you to say.
```

Mediocre Bad Guys

Words and Music by Jack Johnson

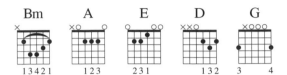

Verse 1

Bm   A |E |
Well, don't give me no comic book sad looks no more.

Bm   A   E |Bm   A |E |
Please don't use those same excuses you've used be - fore, mm, mm.

Bm   A |E |
You told yourself so many times it's o - kay.

Bm   A |E
So eager to try, but you just don't know how to come back down.

Chorus

        ‖Bm
And now you'll beat me up and break me down,

D |
Hoping I don't come around,

A   G |
Kick me when I'm on the ground.

Bm
Beat me up and break me down,

D |
Hoping I don't come around,

A   G   ‖
Kick me when I'm on the ground.

Interlude   **Bm**   **|E**   **|Bm A |E**   **||**

Verse 2

```
Bm                        A
   Well, how about those people?
                   |E
I know that you know  the ones I mean.
       |Bm                 A
Not so good, not so bad, only know what they have,
        |E                                |
And they have only what they've seen, aw.
Bm                   A                      |E        |
   Them mediocre bad  guys can really bring you down.
Bm                   A
   They can't be defeat - ed,
                    |E                              ||
And you know they're nev - er going to come around. They just…
```

Repeat Chorus (3x)

Outro   **Bm   D |A G**   **|**

                Bm   D |A G |Bm   **||**

Mudfootball
(For Moe Lerner)

Words and Music by Jack Johnson

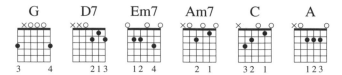

Verse 1

G
Saturday morning and it's time to go.

G
One day these could be the days, but who could have known?

D7
Loading in the back of a pickup truck.

D7
Riding with the boys and pushing the luck.

G
Singing songs loud on the way to the game.

G
Wishing all the things could still be the same.

D7
Chinese homeruns over the backstop.

  |D7
Ko - kua on the ball, and soda pop. Well…

Chorus

Em7   Am7
   We used to laugh a lot,

|C
But only because we thought

    |G   D7 |G   D7 |
That ev - 'rything good always would remain.

G   D7 |G   D7 |
Nothing's gonna change; there's no need to complain.

G | |D7 | ||

Verse 2

G
Sunday morning and it's time to go.

    |G |
Been raining all night so ev'rybody knows.

D7
Over to the field for tackle football.

    |D7 |
Big hits,   big hats, yeah, give me the ball.

G |
Rain is pouring, touchdown scoring.

G |
Keep on rolling, never boring.

D7
Karma, karma, karma chameleon.

    |D7 ||
We're talking kinda funny from helium. Well,

Repeat Chorus

Verse 3

G　　　　　　　　　　　　　　　　　　　|
Monday morning and it's time to go.

G
Wet trunks and schoolbooks and sand on my toes.

　　　|D7
Do an - ything you can to dodge the bus stop blues,

　　　|D7
Like driving a padiddle with a burnt-out fuse.

　　　　　|G
Well, my best friend, Kimi, wants to go with you,

　　|G
So meet her by the sugar mill after school.

　　|D7　　　　　　　　　　　　　　|
My best friend, Kimi, wants to go with you,

D7　　　　　　　　　　　　　　　　　||
Meet her by the sugar mill after school. Well,

Em7　　　　　　**Am7**

Chorus　　　We used to laugh a lot,

　　|C
But only because we thought

　　　　|G　　　　　　**D7**　　　　　**|G**　　　**D7**　　　　　|
That ev - 'rything good always would remain.

Em7　　　　　　**Am7**
　　We used to laugh a lot,

　　|C
But only because we thought

　　　　|A
That ev - 'rything good always would,

　|C　　　　　　　　　　　　　**|G**　　　**D7**
Ev - 'rything good always would remain.

　　　　|G　　**D7**　**|G**　　　　　　||
Mm.

Posters

Words and Music by Jack Johnson

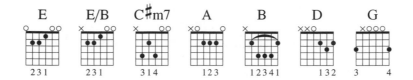

Verse 1

      E   **E/B**
Looking at himself but wishing he was someone else

     |C#m7   **E/B**   **|E E/B |C#m7 E/B**
Because the posters on the wall, they don't look like him at all.

      |E   **E/B**   **|**
So he ties it up, he tucks it in, he pulls it back and gives a grin,

C#m7   **E/B**   **|E E/B |C#m7 E/B**
Laughing at himself because he knows he ain't loved at all.

Chorus

         ‖A
He gets his courage from the can; it makes him feel like a man,

     |B   **|E E/B |C#m7 E/B**
Because he's loving all the ladies but the ladies don't love him at all.

      |A
'Cause when he's not drunk he's only stuck on himself,

     |B   **|E E/B |C#m7 E/B ‖**
And then   he has the nerve to say he needs a decent girl.

Verse 2

```
E                                 E/B
Looking at herself but wishing she was someone else
      |C#m7                       E/B               |E   E/B  |C#m7  E/B
Because the body of the doll, it don't look like hers at all.
      |E                           E/B                              |
So she straps it on, she sucks it in, she throws it up and gives a grin,
C#m7                           E/B                |E   E/B  |C#m7  E/B
Laughing at herself because she knows she ain't that at all.
```

Chorus

```
      ‖A
All caught up in the trends; well, the truth began to bend
      |B                                        |E   E/B  |C#m7  E/B
And the next thing you know, man, there just ain't no truth left at all.
            |A
'Cause when the pretty girl walks, she walks so proud,
            |B                                  |E   E/B  |C#m7  E/B
And when the pretty girl laughs, oh man, she laughs so loud.
```

Bridge

```
      ‖E                   D                       |
And if it ain't this, then it's that. As a matter of fact,
C#m7                      B              |
      She hasn't had a day    to relax
E              D             |
Since she has lost her
C#m7                   |B        |E   E/B  |C#m7 N.C.  |E   E/B  |C#m7  G     A
      Ability to think    clear - ly.
```

Verse 3
```
          ‖E                         E/B                       |
Well, I'm an energetic hypothetic version of another person.
```
```
C♯m7                         E/B                  |E   E/B  |C♯m7  E/B
Check out my outsides; there ain't nothing in here.
```
```
          |E                  E/B                       |
Well, I'm a superficial, systematic, music television addict.
```
```
C♯m7                      E/B
Check out my outsides; there ain't nothing in…
```

Chorus
```
          ‖A                                              |
Here    comes another one, just like the other one.
```
```
B
Looking at himself but wishing he was someone else
```
```
          |E                            E/B              |
Because the posters on the wall, they don't look like him.
```
```
C♯m7                       E/B                        |
Ties   it up, he tucks it in, he pulls it back and gives a grin,
```
```
E                         E/B                          |
Laughing at himself because he knows he ain't loved at all.
```
```
C♯m7     E/B                     |E          ‖
    He  knows he ain't loved at all.
```

Never Know

Words and Music by Jack Johnson

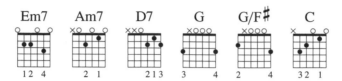

Intro **Em7** |**Am7** |**D7** |**G** **G/F♯** ||

Em7

Verse 1   I heard this old story before,

    |**Am7**

Where the people keep on killing for their metaphors

  |**D7** |**G**   **G/F♯**

But   don't leave much up to the i - magina - tion.

   |**Em7**

So I   wanna give this imagery back,

   |**Am7**

But I   know it just ain't so easy like that.

  |**D7**

So   I turn the page and read the story

  |**G**   **G/F♯** |**C**

A - gain and a - gain and a - gain.

                |**Am**

Sure seems the same

With a different name.

  |**D7**

We're breaking and rebuilding

  |**D7**

And we're growing, always guessing.

Chorus

‖**Em7   Am7**
Never know - ing;

|**D7**   **G**
Shock - ing, but we're noth - ing.

|**Em7 Am7**
We're just mo - ments;

|**D7** |**G**
We're clev - er but we're clue - less.

|**Em7 Am7**
We're just hu - man,

|**D7**   **G**
Amus - ing and confus - ing.

|**Em7 Am7** |**D7**   **G**
We're try - ing, but where   is this all lead - ing?

|**Em7**   **Am7** |**D7** |**G**
We'll never know.

Verse 2

                                   ‖**Em7**
It all happened so much   faster than you could say "disaster."

         |**Am7**
Wanna take a time lapse and look at it backwards,

        |**D7**
Find the last word?

                    |**G**   **G/F♯**
And maybe that's just the answer that we're after.

          |**Em7**
But after all,   we're just a bubble in a boiling pot,

      |**Am7**
Just   one breath in a chain of thought.

       |**D7**
We're moments just combusting;

  |**G**   **G/F♯** |**C**
Feel certain but we'll never, never know.

                |**Am**
Sure seems the same.

Give it a diff'rent name.

    |**D7**
We're begging and we're needing

    |**D7**
And we're trying and we're breathing.

Chorus

```
        ‖Em7     Am7
Never  know - ing;

         |D7                   G
Shock - ing,  but  we're  noth - ing.

         |Em7   Am7
We're  just  mo - ments;

         |D7                   G
We're  clev - er  but  we're  clue - less.

         |Em7  Am7
We're  just  hu  -  man,

      |D7              G
Amus -  ing  and confus - ing.

      |Em7   Am7          |D7                       |G
We're  help -      ing,  we're  build - ing  and  we're  grow - ing.

         |Em7                          |
Never  know.      You  can  never  know,

Am7                 |D7                |G            ‖
   Never  know,        never  know.
```

Verse 3

Em7
    Knock, knock, comin' door to door;

Am7
Tell ya that their metaphor's better than yours.

 |D7
And you can either sink or swim;

G
Things are looking pretty grim.

 |Em7   **|Am7**
If you don't believe in what they're spoon - feeding,

        |D7
It's got no feeling,

              |G   **G/F♯**   **|C**
So I read it again and a - gain and a - gain.

Sure seems the same.

Am7
    So many different names

 |D7
Our hearts are strong; our heads are weak.

 |D7
We'll always be competing.

Chorus

‖**Em7**   **Am7**
Never know - ing;

|**D7**   **G**
Shock - ing, but we're noth - ing.

|**Em7** **Am7**
We're just mo - ments;

|**D7**   **G**
We're clev - er but we're clue - less.

|**Em7** **Am7**
We're just hu   -   man,

|**D7**   **G**
Amus - ing and confus - ing.

|**Em7** **Am7** |**D7**   **G**
But the truth   is,   all we got is ques - tions.

|**Em7** |
We'll never know.   You can never know,

Am7 |**D7** |**G**   ‖
Never know,   never know.

Outro   **Em7** |**Am7** |**D7** |**G** |**Em7**   ‖

The News

Words and Music by Jack Johnson

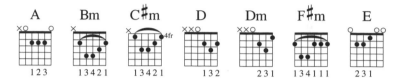

Verse 1

      A   **|Bm** |
A billion people died on the news   tonight,

  A   **|Bm**
But not so many cried at the ter - rible sight.

                      |A |
Well, Mama said, "It's just make believe,

C♯m
      You can't believe everything you see.

 |Bm   **|D**
So baby, close your eyes to the lullabies,

Dm   **|A**   **|Bm**   ‖
On the news   tonight."

STRUM & SING

Verse 2

```
A                                             |Bm            |
Who's the one to decide that it would be      alright,

A                                   |Bm
 To put the music behind the news      tonight?

                    |A                                        |
Well, Mama said,  "You can't believe everything you hear;

C♯m                                 |
    The diagetic world is so unclear.

Bm                              |
    So baby, close your ears

D   C♯m                    |Bm
        On the news tonight,

                        |F♯m
On the news tonight."

    |Bm                                 |
The unobtrusive tones on the news tonight.

F♯m                    |A          |E        ||
    And Mama said, "Mm."
```

Verse 3

```
A                                                    |Bm
Why don't the newscasters cry when they read about people who die?

 |A                                          |Bm
At least they could be decent enough to put just a tear in their eyes.

        |A                       |
Mama said,   "It's just make believe;

C♯m                                 |
    You can't believe everything you see.

 |Bm                              |D
So baby, close your eyes to the lullabies

Dm                |A          |Bm          |A            ||
    On the news   tonight."
```

No Other Way

Words and Music by Jack Johnson

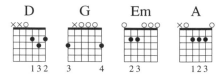

Verse 1

D
   When your mind is a mess,   so is mine.   I can't sleep,

G
  'Cause it hurts when I think.   My thoughts aren't at peace

Em
   With the plans that we make,   chances we take.

G
  They're not yours; they're not mine.   There's waves that can break.

D
  All the words that we said and the words that we mean.

G
   Words can fall short,   can't see the unseen.

Em
   'Cause the world is awake.

         |G
For somebody's sake   now, please close your eyes.

G
  Woman, please get some sleep.

Chorus

```
        D                   |A          G
          And know that if I knew all of the answers,
          |D                             |
        I would    not   hold them from you.
        A           G                    |
        Know all the things that I know;
        D                   |A          G       |Em          |
          We told each other   there is no other   way.
                  |G          |          ‖
        Mm, mm,   mm.
```

Verse 2

```
        D                              |
          Well, too much silence can be   misleading.
          |G                             |
        You're  drifting; I can hear it in the way that you're breathing.
          |Em                         |
        We  don't really need to find rea - son,
                          |G
        'Cause out the same door   that it came,
                  |G               |
        Well, it's leav - ing, it's  leaving.
        D                              |
        Leaving like a day that's done and part of a season.
          |G                            |
        Re - solve is just a concept that's as dead as the leaves,
                  |Em                   |
        But at least   we can sleep.    It's all that we need.
                    |G
        When we wake  we would find,
          |G                               ‖
        Our minds would be free to go to sleep.
```

Repeat Chorus

Rodeo Clowns

Words and Music by Jack Johnson

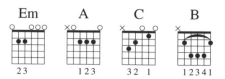

Verse 1

Em
Sweeping the floors, open up the doors, yeah.

A
Turn on the lights, getting ready for tonight.

C
Nobody's romancing 'cause it's too early for dancing,

|**B** ‖
But here comes the music.

Verse 2

Em
Bright lights flashing to cover up your lack of soul.

|**A**
Man - y people, so many problems,

|**C**
So many reasons to buy an - other round; drink it down.

|**B**
Just another night on the town

|**Em**
With the big man, money man, better than the other man.

A
He got the plan with the million dollar give a damn.

C
When nobody understands he'll become a smaller man.

|**B**
The bright lights keep flashing.

Chorus
                                 ‖**Em**   **B**

Women keep on dancing with the clowns, yeah, yeah, yeah.

                         |**C**   **A**

They pick me up when I'm down,   yeah, yeah.

               |**Em**   **B**

The rodeo clowns,   yeah, yeah, yeah,

                       |**C**   **A**   ‖

They pick me up when I'm down.

Verse 3
        ‖**Em**

The disco ball spinning,

                                |**A**

All the music and the women and the shots of tequila.

Man, they say that they need ya.

  |**C**

But what they really need

     |**B**

Is just a little room to breathe.

     |**Em**

Teeny bopping disco queen,

                        |**A**

She barely understands her dreams   of bellybutton rings

                   |**C**

And other kinds of things sym - bolic of change.

But the thing that is strange

     |**B**

Is that the changes occurred.

Chorus

                                             ||Em   B
And now she's just a part of the herd,   yeah, yeah, yeah.

                                 |C   A
Man, I thought that you heard, yeah, yeah.

                    |Em   B
The changes occurred,   yeah, yeah, yeah.

                       |C   A ||
Just a part of the herd.

Verse 4

Em |
Lights out, shut down, late night, wet ground.

A |
 You walk by, look at him, but he can't look at you, yeah.

C |
 You might feel pity, but he only feels the ground.

B |
 You understand moods, but he only knows letdown.

Em |
   By the corner there's another one

A |
Reaching out a hand, coming from a broken man.

     |C |B
Well, you try to live, but he's done trying.   Not dead,

Chorus

                  ||Em
But definitely dying

B |C   A
  With the rest of the clowns,   yeah, yeah.

                      |Em   B
Mm, mm, mm, mm,   mm, mm, mm,

                           |C   A ||
With the rest of the clowns.

Repeat Verse 1

Sitting, Waiting, Wishing

Words and Music by Jack Johnson

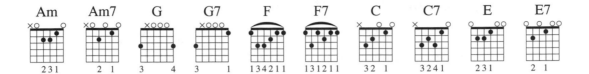

Verse 1

|Am   Am7 |
Well, I   was sitting, waiting, wishing

G   G7 |
You believed in superstitions;

F   F7 |C   C7
Then maybe you'd see the signs.

|Am   Am7
But Lord   knows that this world is cruel,

|G   G7
And I ain't the Lord, no, I'm just a fool,

|F   F7 |C   C7
Learning loving somebody don't make them love you.

Chorus

‖E   E7 |E   E7 |Am   Am7 |Am   Am7
Must I always   be wait - ing, wait - ing on you?

|E   E7 |E   E7 |Am   Am7 |Am   Am7
Must I always   be play - ing, play - ing your fool?

Verse 2

```
 ‖Am                    Am7
I sang your songs, I danced your dance

 |G              G7          |
I gave your friends all a chance.

 F                 F7                    |C      C7
Putting up with them wasn't worth never having you.

   |Am                    Am7
Oh, maybe you've been through this before,

    |G              G7
But it's my first time, so please ignore

         |F              F7          |C      C7
The next  few lines, 'cause they're directed at  you.
```

Chorus

```
        ‖E     E7      |E      E7        |Am   Am7 |Am   Am7
I can't always     be wait - ing, wait - ing on you.

      |E     E7      |E      E7          |Am   Am7 |Am   Am7 ‖
I can't always     be play - ing, play - ing your fool.
```

Bridge

```
C                        |
  I keep playing your part,

E                        |
  But it's not my scene.

F                         |
  Won't this plot not twist?

G         F         |
  I've had e - nough mystery.

C                   |
  Keep building it up,

E                             |
  But then you're shooting me down.

F                      |
  But I'm already down;

G                ‖
  Just wait a minute.
```

Interlude

```
Am    Am7 |G    G7              |
            Just sitting, waiting.

F     F7  |C    C7              |
            Just wait a minute.

Am    Am7 |G    G7              |
            Just sitting, waiting.

F     F7  |C    C7
```

Verse 3

```
          ‖Am         Am7
Well, if I was in your position,

          |G                    G7
I'd put down all my ammunition.

          |F              F7           |C      C7
I'd wonder why it had taken me so  long.

          |Am           Am7
But Lord knows that I'm not you,

          |G                    G7
And if I was, I wouldn't be so cruel,

          |F                    F7     |C      C7
'Cause waiting on love ain't so easy to do.
```

Chorus

```
          ‖E    E7       |E       E7           |Am  Am7 |Am   Am7
Must I always      be wait - ing, wait - ing on you?

          |E    E7       |E       E7           |Am  Am7 |Am   Am7
Must I always      be play - ing, play - ing your fool?

            |E    E7      |E       E7            |Am  Am7 |Am   Am7
No, I can't always      be wait - ing, wait - ing on you.

          |E    E7       |E       E7           |Am Am7   |E E7  |Am      ‖
I can't always      be play - ing, play - ing your fool,        fool.    Mm, mm.
```

Sexy Plexi

Words and Music by Jack Johnson

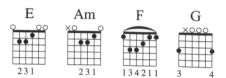

Verse 1

E |**Am** |
Sexy, sexy, made up of plexi dis - asters.

E |
Pushing and pulling, conservative rolling,

Am |
Unlike plastic, easier to see through,

E |
Just like glass with no ring,

Am |
Softer and sadder you sing.

E |
Sexy, sexy, do your thing,

Am |
Learn to be shy and then you can sting.

E |
Plexi, plexi, bend, don't shatter.

F   **G** ||
Once you're broken, shape won't matter.

Chorus

Am   G
   You're breaking your   mind

|F   E
By killing the time that kills   you.

|Am   G
But you can't blame the time,

                  |F   E |Am | ‖
'Cause it's on - ly in your mind.

Verse 2

E
Quickly, quickly grow and then you'll know

                |Am
It's such an awkward show to see.

|E
And everyone you wanted to know

|Am
And everyone you wanted to meet

        |E |Am
Have all   gone away.

             |E |F   G   ‖
Well, they've all   gone away.   And now…

Repeat Chorus

Bridge

Am |E
   You're breaking your mind, you're   breaking your mind.

|Am |E
You're   breaking your mind, you're   breaking your mind.

|Am |E
You're   breaking your mind, you're   breaking your mind.

|Am |E |F   G   ‖
You're   breaking your mind, you're   breaking your mind, mind,   mind.

Outro   Am   G |F   E |Am   G |F   E |Am   ‖

Situations

Words and Music by Jack Johnson

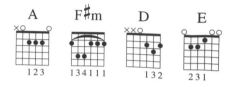

A   F#m   D   E

123   134111   132   231

Intro   **A** |**F#m** |**D** |**E**   **D** ||

Verse

A |
Situation number one,

F#m
It's   the one that's just begun;

|**D** |**E**   **D** |
But   evidently it's too late.

A |
Situation number two,

F#m
It's the only chance for you;

|**D** |**E**   **D** |
It's   controlled by denizens of hate.

A |
Situation number three,

F#m
It's the one that no one sees;

|**D** |**E**   **D** |
It's   all too often dismissed as fate.

A |
Situation number four,

|**F#m**
The one that left you wanting more,

|**D** |**E**   **D** |**A** ||
It,   it tantalized you with its bait.   Oh.

Taylor

Words and Music by Jack Johnson

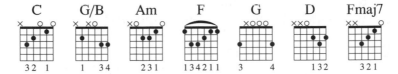

Verse 1

    |C   G/B |
They say Taylor was a good girl, never one to be late,

Am   F |C   G/B |Am   F |
Complain, express ideas in her brain.

C   G/B
Working on the night shift, passing out the tickets;

     |Am   F |C   G/B |Am   F
You're gonna have to pay her if you want to park here.

     |C   G/B |
Well, Mommy's little dancer has quite a little secret;

Am   F |C   G/B |Am   F
Working on the streets now, never gonna keep it.

    |C   G/B
It's quite an imposition and now she's only wishing

   |Am   F |C G/B |Am F ||
That   she would have listened to the words they said.   Poor Taylor.

Chorus

```
      C          G          |Am         F                  |
      She just wanders around,      unaf - fected by

      C        G            |Am       F                    |
       The winter winds, yeah,    and she'll pretend that

      C      G             |Am    F                  |
       She's somewhere else     so far and clear,

      C       G             |Am                       ‖
       About two thousand miles        from here.
```

Interlude

```
      C      G/B   |Am    F    |C      G/B   |Am    F       ‖
```

Verse 2

```
      C                G/B                      |Am         F
      Peter Patrick pit - ter patters on the win - dow,

       |C             G/B            |Am        F          |
      But Sunny Silhouette    won't let him     in.

      C                G/B                      |Am        F
      Poor old Pete's got nothing 'cause he's been falling;

          |C              G/B            |Am       F
      Somehow Sunny knows   just where he's     been.

                        |C                        G/B          |Am    F    |
      He thinks that sing - ing on Sunday's gonna save his soul,

      C     G/B   |Am       F      |
      Now that Saturday's    gone.

      C                G/B          |Am          F
      Sometimes he thinks    that he's on     his way,

                |C      G/B    |Am
      But I could see

            F                      ‖
      That his brake lights are on.
```

Chorus

```
      C         G           |Am         F          |
      He just wanders around,    unaf - fected by

      C    G               |Am    F                  |
      The winter winds, yeah,     and he'll pretend that

      C     G             |Am   F                  |
      He's somewhere else    so far and clear,

      C      G                  |Am                    ‖
      About two thousand miles      from here.
```

Interlude

```
      C     G/B   |Am   F   |C     G/B   |Am   F
```

Verse 3

```
                          ‖C              G/B
      She's such a tough  enchilada filled    up with nada,

      |Am                          F            |C   G/B  |Am    F
      Giv - ing what she gotta give  to get a dollar bill.

            |C                    G/B
      Used to be   a limber chicken; time's    a been a ticking.

      |Am                 F
      Now   she's finger licking to the man

            |C                  G/B
      With the money in his pocket, fly - ing in his rocket,

      |Am                       F               |
      On - ly stopping by on his way to a better world.

      C   D  |F   G                         |
            If Taylor finds a better world,

      C   D  |F     G                      |C        |Fmaj7    ‖
            Then Taylor's gonna run away.
```

Staple It Together

Lyrics by Jack Johnson
Music by Jack Johnson and Merlo Podlewski

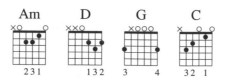

Verse 1

‖Am   D
It's really   too bad.

|Am   D
He became a pris - 'ner of his own past.

|Am   D
He stabbed a mo - ment in the back with a round thumbtack

|Am   D
That held   up the list of things he got to do.

|Am   D
It's really   no good.

|Am   D
He's moving on before he under - stood.

|Am   D
He shot the fu - ture in the foot with ev - 'ry step he took

|Am   D
From the places that he'd been 'cause he forgot to look.

Chorus

‖Am   D |
Better staple it together and call it bad weather.

G   C |
Staple it together and call it bad weather.

Am   D |
Staple it together and call it bad weather.

G   C
Staple it together and call it bad weather.

|Am D |Am D |Am D |Am D
Mm, mm.

Verse 2

        ‖**Am**   **D**
Well, I guess you could say

        |**Am**   **D**
That he don't even know where to be - gin.

              |**Am**   **D**
'Cause he looked   both ways, but he was so afraid,

        |**Am**   **D**
Diggin' deep into the ditch ev - 'ry chance he missed

           |**Am**   **D**
And the mess   he made.

        |**Am**   **D**
'Cause hate is such a strong word.

         |**Am**   **D**
And every brick he laid, a mis - take.

            |**Am**   **D**
They say that his walls   are getting taller, his world is getting smaller.

Repeat Chorus

Repeat Verse 1

Repeat Chorus

Outro

        ‖**Am**   **D** |
If the weather gets better, we should get together.

G   **C**
Spend a little time or we could do whatever.

      |**Am**   **D**
And if we get together we'd be twice as clever.

    |**G**   **C**
So, staple it together and call it bad weather.

      |**Am**   **D** |**G**   **C** |**Am**   **D** |**G**   **C** |**Am**   ‖
Mm, mm.

Symbol in My Driveway

Words and Music by Jack Johnson

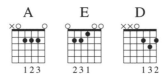

Verse 1

A | |
I've got a symbol in my drive - way.

E | |
I've got a hundred million dollar friends.

D |
I've got you a brand - new weapon.

            |A |E ||
Let's see   how de - structive we can be.

Verse 2

A | |
I've got a brand-new set of sten - cils.

E | |
I been connecting all the dots.

D |
Got my plans in a zip-lock bag.

            |A |E ||
Let's see   how unpro - ductive we can be.

Verse 3

A | |
I've got a light bulb full of an - ger,

E | |
And I can switch it on and off.

D |
In situations it can be so bright.

              |A |E   ‖
I can't believe   how pa - thetic we can be.

Verse 4

A | |
I've got a perfect set of blue - prints.

E | |
I'm gonna build somebody else.

D |
Might cost a little more than money,

|A |E   ‖
But what's man without his wealth?

Verse 5

A | |
I've got a phosphorescent se - cret,

E | |
But don't you tell nobody else.

D |
Next thing you know the whole world   will be talking

|A |E
A - bout all the clues they got. They just ain't no use.

Outro

              ‖A | |E | |
They got fooled.   Mm.

D | |A |E |A   ‖
Mm.   Mm.

Times Like These

Words and Music by Jack Johnson

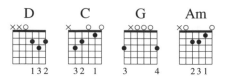

Intro D |C |G |C |G

Verse 1

‖C
In times like   these,

|G
In times like   those,

|C
What will be will be,

|G
And so it goes.

|Am   D |
And it always goes on and on and on and on and on.

Am   D |
On and on and on and on and on it goes.

C |G
   Mm, hmm, hmm.

|C
Mm, hmm, hmm.

|G
Mm, hmm, hmm.

|Am
And there has always been laughing, crying, birth, and dying,

|D
Boys and girls with hearts that take and give and break,

|Am |D
And heal and grow and re-create and raise and nur - ture,

Verse 2   But then hurt from time to times ‖**C** like these,

 |**G**
And times like those.

 |**C**
What will be will be,

 |**G**
And so it goes.

 |**Am**
And there will always be stop and go and fast and slow

 |**D** |
And action, re - action and sticks and stones and broken bones,

Am
Those for peace and those for war,

 |**D**
And God bless these ones, not those ones,

Verse 3   But these ones made times $\|$**C** like these,

            |**G**
And times like   those.

                 |**C**
What will be will be,

            |**G**
And so it goes.

                |**Am**   **D**
And it always goes on and on and on and on and on.

        |**Am**   **D** |
And on   and on and on and on and on it goes.

C |**G**
  Mm, hmm, hmm.

         |**C**
Mm, hmm, hmm.

         |**G**
Mm, hmm, hmm.

             |**Am** |**G**
But somehow I   know it won't be the same.

           |**Am** |**G** $\|$
Somehow I   know (it'll) never be the same.

Tomorrow Morning

Words and Music by Jack Johnson

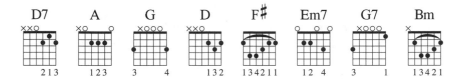

Intro

|D7
Well, that's all right,   if that's all right.

A |G
    Two thousand miles,   but still that's all right.

D7
And that's all right,   if that's all right.

A |G |D7
    I'll see you in the morn - ing, if that's all right.

Verse 1

D   F#
What would you do if I wrote   you a song?

    |Em7   A
Would you give me some loving when I get home?

    |D
Or would you be mad at me

    F# |Em7
If I had   a hard time getting a hold of you?

    |G7
I try all the time.

Chorus

```
        D         Bm   |Em7                      A                            |D        Bm        |
        I'll bet that         you don't know any - body that could be   so bad.
        Em7                   A                            |D        Bm        |
             But if you did,    you'd be wondering where   I'm at.
        Em7                       A                         ‖
        I'll be home when to - morrow morning comes.
```

Interlude

```
        D       F♯    |Em7    A      |

        D       F♯    |Em7    A      ‖
```

Verse 2

```
        D                              F♯
        What would you do if I sang    you this song?

                  |Em7                     A
        The con - nection is bad, but that's only the phone.

                        |D
        'Cause when my words kiss your ear,

        F♯                    |Em7
        I'll be right there. The message is long,

                  |G7                     ‖
        'Cause baby, this is your song.
```

Chorus

```
        D          Bm  |Em7                    A                      |D        Bm      |
```
I'll bet, bet   you don't know any - body that could be   so bad.

```
Em7                 A                       |D        Bm      |
```
  But if you did,   you'd be wondering where   I'm at.

```
Em7                        A
```
I'll be home when to - morrow morning…

```
   |D          Bm  |Em7                    A                      |D        Bm |
```
And I'll bet, bet   you don't know any - body that could be   so bad.

```
Em7                 A                       |D        Bm      |
```
  But if you did,   you'd be wondering where   I'm at.

```
Em7                        A                        |
```
I'll be home when to - morrow morning…

```
D                  Bm
```
  And that's all right,

```
   |Em7                    A                      |
```
'Cause I'll be home when to - morrow morning…

```
D             Bm
```
  And that's all   right,

```
   |Em7                    A                      |D           ‖
```
'Cause I'll be home when to - morrow morning comes.

Traffic in the Sky

Words and Music by Jack Johnson

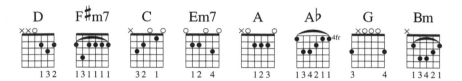

Verse 1

    D   **F♯m7**
There's traffic in the sky

                |C   **Em7**
And it doesn't seem to be getting much better.

                |D
There's kids playing games on the pavement,

    F♯m7   **|**
Drawing waves on the pavement, mm, hmm;

C   **Em7**   **|**
    Shadows of the planes on the pavement, mm, hmm.

D   **F♯m7**
 It's enough to make me cry,

                |C   **Em7**
But that don't seem like it would make it feel better.

                |D
Maybe it's a dream and if I scream

    F♯m7
It will burst at the seams.

                |C   **Em7**
(The) whole place would fall into piec - es,

                |A   **A♭**   **||**
And then they'd say...

Chorus

    G   **A**
  "Well, how could we have known?"

             |**D**   **Bm**
I'll tell them it's not   so hard to tell.

    |**G**   **A**
No, no, no. If you keep adding stones,

       |**D**   **Bm**
Soon the water will be lost in the well.

   |**G**   **A**   ‖
Mm, hmm.

Verse 2

  D   **F♯m7**
  Puzzle pieces in the ground;

  |**C**   **Em7**
No one ever seems to be digging.

             |**D**
Instead they're looking up towards the heavens

    F♯m7 |
With their eyes on the heavens, mm, hmm;

C   **Em7** |
  There're shadows on the way to the heavens, mm, hmm.

D   **F♯m7**
  It's enough to make me cry,

      |**C**   **Em7**
But that don't seem like it would make it feel better.

       |**D**
The answers could be found.

          F♯m7
We could learn from digging down,

    |**C**   **Em7**
But no one ever seems to be dig - ging.

       |**A**   **A♭** ‖
Instead they'll say…

Repeat Chorus

Verse 3

```
D                           F#m7
Words of wisdom all a - round,
        |C                    Em7
But no   one ever seems to listen.
                             |D
They're talking 'bout their plans on the paper,
        F#m7                              |
Building up    from the pavement, mm, hmm;
C                          Em7                            |
  There're shadows from the scrapers on the pavement, mm, hmm.
D                         F#m7
  It's enough to make me sigh,
            |C                          Em7
But that don't seem like it would make it feel better.
            |D
The words are all a - round,
            F#m7
But the words are only sounds,
        |C                    Em7
And no   one ever seems to lis - ten.
            |A             Ab  ‖
Instead, they'll say…
```

Chorus

```
G                           A
"Well, how could we have known?"
                  |D                Bm
I'll tell them it's really not so hard to tell.
        |G                          A
No, no, no. If you keep adding stones,
        |D              Bm
Soon the water will be lost in the well,
        |G      A      |D              ‖
Lost in the well. Mm,   mm, mm, mm.
```

Wasting Time

Words and Music by
Jack Johnson, Merlo Podlewski and Adam Topol

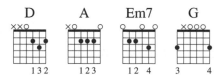

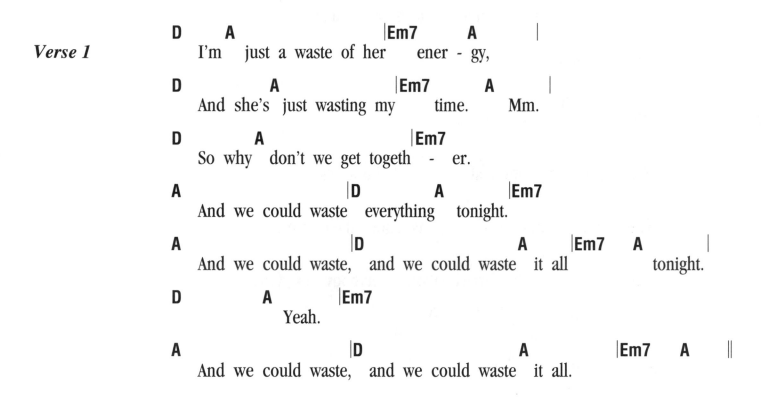

Verse 2

```
D        A                      |Em7      A        |
     I don't  pretend to know what you know.   No, no.

D            A                  |Em7             A          |
     Now, please   don't pretend to know     what's on my mind.

D         A              |Em7                    A
     If we al - ready knew everything    that everybody knows,

          |D            A         |Em7      A
We would have  nothing to learn   tonight.

              |D         A        |Em7      A
And we would have   nothing to show tonight.
```

Chorus

```
          ‖G
Oh, but ev - 'rybody thinks

                       |A
That everybody knows about ev - 'rybody else.

              |G
(But) nobody knows an - ything about themselves,

         |A                                |
'Cause they're   all worried about everybody else, yeah.

D      A      |Em7     A        |
     Yeah.            Mm.

D      A      |Em7     A        ‖
          Oh.
```

Verse 3

D   A |Em7   A |
Love's   just a waste of our   ener - gy, yeah,

D   A |Em7   A |
And this life's   just a waste of our   time.

D   A |Em7
So why   don't we get togeth - er?

A |D   A |Em7
And we could waste   everything   tonight.

A |D   A |Em7
And we could waste,   and we could waste   it all.

Chorus

A   ‖G
Yeah, but ev - 'rybody thinks

                       |A
That everybody knows about ev - 'rybody else.

                 |G
No, no, nobody knows an - ything about themselves,

     |A |
'Cause they're   all worried about everybody else, yeah.

D   A |Em7   A |
   Oh.

D   A |Em7   A   ‖
    And we could waste…

Outro

D   A |
Do, do, do, do, do, do, do.

Em7   A |
Do, do, do, do, do, do, do, do, do, do, do.

D   A |
Do, do, do, do, do, do, do.

Em7   A |D   ‖
Do, do, do, do, do, do, do, do, do, do, do, do, do.

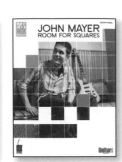